The Humble Administrator's Garden

VIKRAM SETH

The Humble Administrator's Garden

CARCANET

First published in 1985 by
Carcanet Press Ltd
208-212 Corn Exchange Buildings
Manchester M4 3BQ

Copyright © Vikram Seth 1985

British Library Cataloguing in Publication Data

Seth, Vikram
    The humble administrator's garden.
    I. Title
    821   PR9499.3.S34/

    ISBN 0-85635-583-6

The Publisher acknowledges financial assistance
from the Arts Council of Great Britain

Typeset by Bryan Williamson, Swinton, Berwickshire
Printed in England by SRP Ltd., Exeter

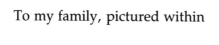

To my family, pictured within

Contents

Wutong

A Little Night Music

White walls. Moonlight. I wander through
The alleys skein-drawn by the sound
Of someone playing the erhu.
A courtyard; two chairs on the ground.

As if he knew I'd come tonight
He gestures, only half-surprised.
The old hands poise. The bow takes flight
And unwished tears come to my eyes.

He pauses, tunes, and plays again
An hour beneath the wutong trees
For self and stranger, as if all men
Were brothers within the enclosing seas.

Suzhou, 1981

The Master-of-Nets Garden

Magnolia petals fall, pale, fragrant, brown,
Resting on moss within a square of white;
Courtyard of quietness, of intimate stone
And latticed shadow. Outside, low at night,
Three moons — of water, mirror, sky — define
Pine and old cypress struggling against the stars,
And jasmine and gardenia combine
Their scent with that of closed magnolias.

The Humble Administrator's Garden

A plump gold carp nudges a lily pad
And shakes the raindrops off like mercury,
And Mr Wang walks round. "Not bad, not bad."
He eyes the Fragrant Chamber dreamily.
He eyes the Rainbow Bridge. He may have got
The means by somewhat dubious means, but now
This is the loveliest of all gardens. What
Do scruples know of beauty anyhow?
The Humble Administrator admires a bee
Poised on a lotus, walks through the bamboo wood,
Strips half a dozen loquats off a tree
And looks about and sees that it is good.
  He leans against a willow with a dish
  And throws a dumpling to a passing fish.

The North Temple Tower

On the North Temple Tower, from the fifth floor
I pull fierce faces at two boys below.
One gasps, and tells the other what he saw:
A waibin in the throes of vertigo.
They look again. I spread my arms and grunt.
Sudden delight: they point upwards and scowl.
One imitates a baby elephant.
The other glares and totters like an owl.
The camera clicks. They do not seem to mind
Involuntary immortality.
I change a reel, and spiral down to find
Them stomping through the flower-beds with glee.
  They say "Ni hao", remembering their manners,
  Then leap away through hollyhocks and cannas.

The Gentle Waves Pavilion

A pool as green as pea-soup. Four sleek fish,
Red as pimentos, push through bubbly scum.
A vagrant sparrow from a rocky niche
Looks critically on. Two lovers come
To gaze at fish and foreigner in the park
And talk and cuddle by the moss-trunked tree
And with a pen-knife hack their names through bark
For (if the tree survives) posterity.

The Tarrying Garden

Here are no vistas. Piece by piece unfolds.
Stand by the rock. The lotus and the fish,
In still pale yellows, greens and fluid golds
Startle the rainy sky. Or if you wish
Stare at a single slab of cursive script
Sealed in the whitewash, passionate, bone-strong,
Crafted, uncrafted, singular, and stripped
Of all superfluous charm. Or walk along
The covered walks, the courtyards and the pools,
The zigzags of embodied hesitation,
A strict game where, within the given rules
You may throw dice or follow inclination.
  The Tarrying Garden, piecemeal or entire:
  Meander, tarry, amble, pause, admire.

The Great Confucian Temple, Suzhou

Two geese strut through the balustrade, where rust
And stacks of timber marked "Department of
Culture: for Restoration" gather dust.
The ginkgo lodges a complaining dove.
A centipede squirms over "Hong Wu" hewn
In seal-script on the white fragmented stone
Where reign-names of the Ming and Qing lie strewn
In mint and dog-turd, creeper, tile and bone.
Before the frayed vermilion walls and eaves
The plaster statue of a man in red
With pudgy vehemence and rolled-up sleeves
Proclaims the oppressive heritage is dead.
  Inside the hall six workmen renovate
  The verveless splendour of a corpse of state.

Nanjing Night

Full moon, the Nanjing walls, bicycle bells.
Two children huddle in the 10 o'clock movie crowd
Against the plunging cold. The air foretells
Snow, moonlit snow. Low-voiced, dog-eared, heads bowed,
Students seep out from libraries into the cold.
It is the last month — the yellow plum is in bloom.
Exams, the Spring Festival; each one is to be told
His lifework by the Party. In the room
Someone grinds his teeth in his sleep and moans.
The moonlight finds two pink hot-water flasks,
Pull-up bars, a leafless ginkgo, four stones —
Either the Gang of Four or the Four Great Tasks.
    I dream of the twelve full moons of the coming year:
    Tilts of curved roof; branches; a stonewhite sphere.

Evening Wheat

Evening is the best time for wheat.
Toads croak.
Children ride buffaloes home for supper.
The last loads are shoulder-borne.
Squares light up
And the wheat sags with a late gold.
There on the other side of the raised path
Is the untransplanted emerald rice.
But it is the wheat I watch, the still dark gold
With maybe a pig that has strayed from the brigade
Enjoying a few soft ears.

The Accountant's House

We go in the evening to the accountant's house.
It is dark and the road is slush.
The fireflies fleck silver.
The ash flicked off by my companion, the barefoot doctor, is gold.

I want to clear up some questions on the income and expenditure
    account.
His wife and two daughters smile as I come in.
They pour tea. Their son died last Spring Festival.
We smile and discuss electricity fees.

This is my last day here. The Ministry of Education
Has decreed a two-and-a-half-week limit.
I will turn into a pumpkin soon enough
But today there is work, are pleasantries.

The green seedlings outside have been transplanted.
The accountant looks sad and my heart goes out.
No-one knows how he died. He came home from play
And his head was hot, his nose bled, and he died.

Yet they laugh, yet they laugh, these lovely people,
And he clicks his abacus and she gives me a towel and the two
    girls
Smile shyly, boldly at the stranger and the father
Discussing matters of much importance together.

Research in Jiangsu Province

From off this plastic strip the noise
Of buzzing stops. A human voice
Asks its set questions, pauses, then
Waits for responses to begin.

The questions bore in. How much is
The cost and area of this house?
I see you have two sons. Would you
Prefer to have had a daughter too?

And do your private plots provide
Substantial income on the side?
Do you rear silkworms? goslings? pigs?
How much per year is spent on eggs?

How much on oil and soya sauce
And salt and vinegar? asks the voice.
The answering phantom states a figure,
Then reconsiders, makes it bigger.

Children and contraceptives, soap
And schooling rise like dreams of hope
To whirl with radios and bikes
Round pensions, tea and alarm clocks.

"Forty square metres. Sixteen cents.
To save us from the elements.
Miscarriage. Pickle with rice-gruel
Three times a week. Rice-straw for fuel.

Chickens and fruit-trees." In Jiangning
Green spurts the psychedelic Spring
And blossoming plum confounds the smell
Of pig-shit plastered on the soil.

Life and production, drought and flood
Merge with the fertile river mud
And maids come forth sprig-muslin drest
And mandarin ducks return to nest.

The Yangtse flows on like brown tape.
The research forms take final shape,
Each figure like a laden boat
With white or madder sails afloat.

Float on, float on, O facts and facts,
Distilled compendia of past acts,
Reveal the Grand Design to me,
Flotilla of my PhD.

On the obnoxious dreary pillage
Of privacy, imperfect knowledge
Will sprout like lodged rice, rank with grain,
In whose submerging ears obtain

Statistics where none grew before
And housing estimates galore,
Diet and wealth and income data,
Age structures and a price inflator,

Birth and fertility projections,
Plans based on need and predilections.
O needful numbers, and half true,
Without you what would nations do?

I switch the tape off. This to me
Encapsulates reality,
Although the beckoning plum-trees splayed
Against the sky, the fragrant shade,

Have something tellable, it seems,
Of evanescence, light and dreams,
And the cloud-busy, far-blue air
Forms a continuous questionnaire

And Mrs Gao herself whose voice
Is captive on my tape may choose
Some time when tapes and forms are far
To talk about the Japanese War,

May mention how her family fled,
And starved, and bartered her for bread,
And stroke her grandson's head and say
Such things could not occur today.

From a Traveller

The willows cut across the commune fields.
Smoke pours from stacks across persimmon trees.
The afternoon light and the jolt of the rails
Provoke the familiar nostalgia of travellers
As I read your letter (thank you for writing) once and again,
And sip warm water from my cup and think of what to say.

Thank you for writing (again) and for the poem.
It came a week ago and has been with me since.
It made me happy. It is very fine —
Latinate and resonant, the words precisely hefted.
As for craft, rhyme and metre are well
But this has more, a balanced power.
I want to know if the proximity
Of "obvious", "obtuse" and "obscure" was meant or not
To be an obtrusive touch of humour or skill,
Though of course my professional opinion is not what you require
So much as an explication of my status
As amateur.

Returning from a journey of some length
From the Southern to the Northern capital, my mind turns
To Nanjing in its Fall loveliness
With the Ming tomb before the wooded knoll,
The acorns, chestnuts and small sprouts of oak
On the unneedled ground beneath the pines
And a few pine-rats (squirrels) scampering around
As if to reconfirm that there are few places here
To be solitary, and I realise that I
Go around the world gathering as much
Nostalgia as knowledge, for I can see that no sooner
Will I have moved to an Eccentric State
Than the whole weight of the Central Kingdom
Will ravage my memory — the rasp and swash
Of the catalpa trees, the oversize magpies, my friends,
The pleasure of walking the lanes of a poor country

Where there is no or little destitution,
This afternoon sun and these persimmon orchards
And the clank of rails, and so I often fear
That those few days we spent in each other's company
In San Francisco in the imperial months
And those nights were just another part
Of a tenuous tissue, real enough at the time
Yet changeable as the sieved light that falls
Upon this page from beyond the embanked trees
And so though I was happy it revived my disquiet
To know you thought as much about those days
As I.

When you go to The Latest Scoop next time ·
Buy chocolate-chocolate-chip in honour of me.
I imagine you there as often as in
Bed or the studio or your roach-frequented kitchen
(I remember you in tastes — ice-cream, garlic soup,
Cinnamon rolls, pâté) and at alternate chips
Mumble "obtuse" and "not obtuse" and tell me the result
(And if the latter overtip the friendly giant)
For the obtuseness you diagnosed with such acuity
Had in it an element of intention.
Apart from the aspect of physical difference,
As exciting to me as that of similarity,
And beauty that I always am a sucker for,
I loved in you that cavalier, ungiving
Self-inwardness I usually link with men,
And I suppose it worried me, this affinity and ours —
To what end should any inklings be confirmed
To be uprooted in a predictable week?
What if within this year, what if, what if
You or I were to find the all-gold baby,
Compleat and mechanical, with whom we wished
To play at birds and orchids all our life,
How would we face each other when I returned
Or revive those Vivaldian Beach-Boyish days,
Endless Summer — the most nostalgic of the seasons

For sunspoilt denizens of the Old Gold Mountain
As is Spring in the City of Dreaming Spires,
Winter in Delhi, or here by the Great River
The long slow-cooling cycles of a temperate Fall.
The fact that those days were is perhaps enough.
Time tempers natures, true; but they have existed.
Though all of it, Han, Tang, Song, Ming, Qing,
Their turbulence and life have left few marks
Upon the physical city of Nanjing
And even its tragic century is unreflected
Except for younger brick where the Qing mined in
To crush the Heavenly Kingdom of Great Peace
Or there the mausoleum of Sun Zhong Shan —
And the Guomindang killings and the Japanese horror
Are of less permanence than the coeval plane-trees
That string the streets, still it has been. I feel
Acknowledgement could not add weight to it,
Still less to the levity and gravity of our bond.
Why tax our urban idyll with admission when we,
Both of us, wish, more than we need commit
To meet and spend more than those countable days
In the repeatable magic of San Francisco?
I am honing my charm. For the interim
Though with you I basked perhaps too unfeelingly in
The luxury of not needing to compromise,
And most of what I say is still inchoate
Or irrelevant or evasive, take at least
The "I like you" you once skilfully prised from me
As indefensible and true.

A Little Distance

A little distance from the waterfall
By a small pool the yellow beachtowel lies
On a long warm rock, and near it azaleas grow
And the shadows of thin fish fall
Across the speckled stones, and a light breeze blows
Rippling the skin of the pool, first this way, then that.
A blue-tailed lizard suns itself
And we ourselves as the sun burns through a cloud
Into the secluded valley, onto the pool,
Onto the rocks, into our cold bones.

Tired, tired, my mind melts in the sun.
An ant crawls over my ankle. I sit up: there
You lie, beautiful, half-nude on the white pebbles,
Cream-coloured breasts open to the breeze and the sky
And a few lines of silver hair in the brown
To announce the burden of your twenty-eight years.
To be chaste, how frustrating for minutes,
How uncomplicated for days — to order fish, chives,
To discuss the rats in our room when the morning gongs
Sound out the monastery routine. To be
Just friends, reverting in a richer vein
To what we were, the way that we once were,
The way I hope, for a while, we may remain.

After six days, with nothing voiced, we are
Unexpectant, companionable,
Perhaps like an aging couple. We do not
Even kiss goodnight yet wake to friendliness.
It is perhaps the tiredness in my mind
Or the fear of a structure set. Unsettledness
Is what I have come to fear. We sit away
From the noise of the waterfall, by a clear pool,
Less conscious of the risk that is not worthwhile

Than of the warm grey boulders and the slopes
That circumscribe our peace, and the warmth of the sun
Melting us into the stones, and the azaleas
Mauve against a sea of pine.

A Hangzhou Garden

Wistaria twigs, wistaria leaves, mauve petals
Drift past a goldfish ripple. As it settles
Another flower drops. Below, redly,
The fish meander through the wistaria tree.

From an "East is Red" Steamer

The old man in grey reproves the women's tears
And shouts from dock to deck. The sailor hears,
Smiles, flings a cigarette to a shorebound mate.
The Wuhan steamer hoots — two minutes late —
Plays martial music, exhorts us to do more
For the Four Modernisations, moves from shore,
While I the tourist view the mother and daughter
Waving across the broadening rift of water,
The grey and sunflecked water and the seagulls flying
Between the son and father, who now himself is crying.

Neem

Profiting

Uncomprehending day,
I tie my loss to leaves
And watch them drift away.

The regions are as far,
But the whole quadrant sees
The single generous star.

Yet under star or sun,
For forest tree or leaf
The year has wandered on.

And for the single cells
Held in their sentient skins
An image shapes and tells:

In wreathes of ache and strain
The bent rheumatic potter
Constructs his forms from pain.

The They

They have left me the quiet gift of fearing.
I am consumed by fear, chilling and searing.

I shiver at night. I cannot sleep. I burn
By night, by day. I tremble. They return.

They bear an abstract laser to destroy
Love-love and Live-live, little girl and boy.

Thus my heart jolts in fear. For they are known
To liquidate the squealers, sparing none.

Needless to say, the death is always long.
I weep to think of it; I am not strong.

Who are the They? Why do they act this way?
Some of us know, but no-one dares to say.

The Comfortable Classes at Work and Play

A squirrel crawls on top of Ganesh.
Oscar turns over on his stomach and rolls about.
Seven satbhai-champas chatter and burble below the bignonia
     trellis.
The raat-ki-rani and malati and harsingar mingle their scent.
Above, two crows on the eaves upset Divali diyas on the ground,
And in the evening a hoopoe pecks at the lawn
While mynahs frolic at the edge of the mango's shade
And parrots flash across the sky.

Early in the morning the mew-like wail
Of peacocks from the grounds of Nehru's old house,
Now the Teenmurti Library, comes down the lanes,
And down the lanes and across the garden hedges
The peacocks themselves, turquoise-necked, turquoise-breasted
(With tail-feathers all robbed to make peacock fans)
Walk primly to our neighbours' houses and ours
Conducting a progress through the vegetable garden.

Sona the gardener does not chase them out
From by the banana tree and the gourd-vines.
He prunes the roses, the hedge, the champa, the two
Lantana elephants that welcome walkers in
To walk, after drinking ginger tea against the chill,
In chappals on the dew-soft dew-greyed lawn
Or to sit on the large white swing
And swing and stare or read.

The eldest son brings down his surpeti
And mumbles a snatch of Lalit, then hums and lapses.
Oscar bores out of the hedge from the neighbour's garden
And hurls himself barking at the singer's feet.
The eldest son says, "No, Oscar, no!"
But is persuaded by a sequence of short nips
To run Oscar down the red path
As far as the whitewashed gate.

The second son brings down *The Women's Room*,
Of Woman Born, *My Mother/My Self* and *Sexual Politics*.
His girl-friend is feminist, and he is feminist.
When his girl-friend was anarchist, he was anarchist.
He has begun of late to talk in psychobabble
And his elder brother does not improve energy interflows
By cynical imitation of his style of speech
Or cynical puncturing of his current ism.

The daughter of the house sits in her room
Immersed in sociology and social visits
Paid her at any hour by many friends,
And talks about their coming field-trip south
Where they, like earlier cohorts from their college
("A shock of sociologists") will examine
The much-examined customs of the Todas
(Who have learned now to exploit their data-pickers).

In the long sunlit closed verandah
The mother takes a volume in half-calf
From off the wall, and wrestles with a judgment
Of Justice Krishna Iyer of the Supreme Court.
He must mean something, but what does he mean?
"The endless pathology of factious scrimmage" — and now
"Crypto-coercion". She knits her forehead
And asks for another cup of ginger tea.

The father sits in bed reading the *Indian Express*,
Inveighing against politicians and corruption.
"India could do so much . . ." he says.
"Even in the time of the British . . ." he says.
"Can you believe it — on every bag of cement —
And still he continues to be a minister!
The rot has gone too deep. Let's go for a walk."
He and the elder son drive to Lodi Gardens.

34

There against the exquisite morning sky
The Arab domes of the tombs sit formed and fine
And neem and semal, ashok and amaltas
And casuarina lend the air freshness, the heart peace.
On the enamel-striped domes the vultures nest.
Along the casual paths three joggers thump.
A group of eight old citizens wearing safas
Gossip in the growing sun and laugh with abandon.

At home the grandmother has sat down to breakfast
And complains that she is ignored, unloved.
Her blood pressure is high, her spirits low.
She is not allowed to eat gulabjamuns.
The doctor has compiled an Index of Foods
And today, to compound things, is a non-grain fast.
Her dentures hurt. She looks at a stuffed tomato
And considers how to darn her grandson's sweater.

The Gift

Awake, he recalls
The district of his sleep.
It was desert land,
The dunes gold, steep,
Warm to the bare foot, walls
Of pliant sand.

Someone, was he a friend?,
Placed a stone of jade
In his hand
And, laughing, said
"When this comes to an end
You will not understand."

He is awake, yet through
The ache of light
He longs to dream again.
He longs for night,
The contour of the sand, the rendezvous,
The gift of jade, of sight.

Homeless

I envy those
Who have a house of their own,
Who can say their feet
Rest on what is theirs alone,
Who do not live on sufferance
In strangers' shells,
As my family has all our life,
And as I probably will.

A place on the earth, untenured,
Soil, grass, brick, air;
To know I will never have to move;
To review the seasons from one lair.
When night comes, to lie down in peace;
To know that I may die as I have slept;
That things will not revert to a stranger's hand;
That those I love may keep what I have kept.

From the Babur-Nama
Memoirs of Babur, First Moghul Emperor of India

1.

A lad called Baburi lived in the camp-bazaar.
Odd how our names matched. I became fond of him —
"Nay, to speak truth, distracted after him."
I had never before this been in love
Or witnessed words expressive of passion, but now
I wrote some Persian verses: "Never was lover
So wretched, so enamoured, so dishonoured
As I"; and others of this type. Sometimes
Baburi came to see me, and I, Babur,
Could scarcely look him in the face, much less
Talk to him, amuse him, or disclose the matter
Weighing on me. So joyful was I I could not
Thank him for visiting; how then could I
Reproach him for departing? I lacked even
The self-command to be polite to him.
Passing one day through a narrow lane with only
A few companions, suddenly, face to face,
I met him, and I almost fell to pieces.
I could not meet his eyes or say a word.
Shame overcame me. I passed on, and left him,
And Muhammed Salih's verses came to my mind —
"I am abashed whenever I see my love.
My friends look at me; I look another way."

This passion in my effervescent youth
Drove me through lane and street, bare-foot, bare-headed,
Through orchard, vineyard, neglecting the respect
And attention due both to myself and to others:
"During my passion I was deranged, nor knew that
Such is the state of one who is in love."
Sometimes, afflicted, I would roam alone
Over the mountains and deserts, sometimes I wandered

From street to street, in suburbs and in gardens.
"To such a state did you reduce me, O heart — "
I could not stand or walk; remain or go.

2.

At dawn we left the stream and resumed our march.
I ate a maajun. Under its effect
I visited some gardens, dense with yellow
And purple flowers; some beds yellow, some purple,
And some so intermingled — sprung up together
As if they had been flung and scattered abroad.
I sat down on a hillock. On every side
The gardens lay before me, shaped into beds,
Yellow on one side, purple on another,
Laid out in hexagons, exquisitely.

On Saturday we had a drinking party.
The following day, when we had nearly arrived
At Khwajeh Sehyaran, a serpent was killed,
As thick as an arm, as long as two outstretched.
Out of this large one crept a thinner one,
Yet all its parts were sound and quite uninjured;
Out of this thinner serpent came a mouse,
Perfectly sound again, with no limb injured.
(When we arrived, we had a drinking party.)

Hindustan is a land of meagre pleasures.
The people are not handsome, nor have they
The least conception of the charms of friendship.
They have no spirit, no comprehension, kindness
Or fellow-feeling — no inventiveness
In handicraft or skill in design — no method,
Order, principle, rule in work or thought;
No good flesh or bread in their bazaars,
No ice, cold water, musk-melons, grapes; no horses;
No aqueducts or canals in palace or garden,
Not a single bath or college in the whole land,
No candles, no torches; not even a candlestick.

A splendid bird, more known for colour and beauty
Than bulk, is the peacock. Its size is that of the crane.
The head of the male has an iridescent lustre;
His neck is a fine blue, his back is rich
With yellows, violets, greens and blues, and stars
Extend to the very extremity of his tail.
The bird flies badly, worse indeed than the pheasant:
Where peacocks choose to live, jackals abound.
The doctrines of Hanifeh state that the bird
Is lawful food, its flesh quite pleasant, quail-like;
But eaten somewhat with loathing — like that of the camel.

The frogs of Hindustan are worthy of notice.
Although their species is the same as ours,
They will run seven yards on the face of the water.

3.

Noblemen and soldiers — every man
Who comes into this world is subject to
Dissolution. When we pass away
God alone survives, unchangeable.
Whoever tastes the feast of life must drink
The cup of death. The traveller at the inn
Of mortality sooner or later leaves
That house of sorrow, the world. Is it not better
To die with honour than live with infamy?
"With fame, even to die makes me content.
Let me have fame, since Death has my body."
The Most High God has been propitious to us
For we are placed in such a crisis that
Should we now die we die the death of martyrs
And should we live we will have served his cause.
Let us all swear then not to turn from battle
Nor desert the slaughter ensuing until we die.

4.

To Humayun, whom I long to see; much health.
On Saturday your letters came from the Northwest.
Praise be to God, who has given you a child;
To you a child, to me an object of love
And comfort. You name him Al Amaan. Consider,
"The protected" — Al Amaan — is pronounced by some
Alaaman, which means "plunderer" in our tongue!
Well, may God prosper his name and constitution;
May he be happy, and we made happy by
The fame and fortune of Al Amaan. Indeed
God from his grace and bounty has accomplished
Most unprecedentedly all our desires.

On the eleventh I heard the men of Balkh
Had opened the city. I sent word to your brother
And to the Begs to join you against Merv,
Hissar or Samarkand as you deem fittest,
That through God's mercy you might be enabled
To scatter the enemy, seize their lands, and make
Your friends rejoice in their discomfiture.
This is the time to expose yourself to danger.
Exert yourself, and meet things as they come,
For indolence suits ill with royalty.
If through God's favour Balkh and Hissar are ours,
You rule Hissar; let Kamran be in Balkh.
If Samarkand should fall, it falls to you.
Six parts are always yours, and five Kamran's;
Remember this; the great are generous.

I have a quarrel with you. Your letters are
Illegible. They take hours to decode —
The writing crabbed, the style, too, somewhat strange.
(A riddle is not normally written in prose.)
The spelling is not bad (though *iltafaat*
Is spelt with *te* not *toeh*); yet even when read
The far-fetched diction you delight in veils
Your meaning. This is affectation. Write

From now on, clearly, using words that cost
Less torment both to your reader and to you.

In several of your letters you are saddened
By separation from your friends. Consider —
"If you are independent, follow your will.
If circumstances fetter you, submit."
There is no bondage greater than a king's.
Of this, my son, do not therefore complain.

This letter goes to you with Bian Sheikh
Who will tell you much else by word of mouth.
Maintain the army's discipline and force.
Farewell. The thirteenth day of the first Rabi.

5.

Humayun left Badakhshan after a year,
Journeying via Kabul to Agra to see me.
He sent no word. His mother and I were talking
Of him when he appeared. His presence made
Our hearts blossom like rosebuds, and our eyes shine
Like torches. It had been my daily custom
To hold an open table, yet when he arrived
I threw a feast in his honour and treated him
In both a distinguished and most intimate manner.
The truth is that his conversation held
An inexpressible charm, and he realised
For me the very type of the perfect man.

When the time came Humayun took his leave
To go to Sambhal, his appointed seat,
Where he remained six months. He became ill.
The climate did not suit him. Fever attacked him
And worsened daily. I ordered that he be brought
To Agra, so the best doctors might prescribe
Some treatment. He travelled by water several days.
Despite the remedies he got no better.
His life was despaired of. I was in despair

Till Abdul Kasim said, "In such a case
A sacrifice of great value may incline God
To restore the patient's health." Nothing was dearer
Than his life save my own. I offered it.
My friends protested, saying the great diamond
That came to me with Agra would suffice.
I entered the chamber where my son was lying
And circled his bed three times, saying each time,
"I take upon myself all that you suffer."
I forthwith felt myself depressed and heavy
And in much pain. He rose in perfect health.
I called my noblemen. Placing their hands
In Humayun's as a mark of investiture,
I proclaimed him heir and placed him on the throne.
Those there concurred, and bound themselves to serve him.

Live-Oak

Curious Mishaps

As I was clipping my nails out in the yard
A squirrel came to take a look at me.
He twitched his rat-like face, stared at me hard,
Raised his right paw with smart solemnity

And placed it on his chest, as if on oath.
From a live-oak against the twilight sky
An owl swooped downwards to survey us both,
Judged distances, and with a hybrid cry —

Half dog, half pigeon — fell upon his prey.
The squirrel had no chance, being far from cover.
Incurious, he would have got away.
One hoot: one squeak; and things were quickly over.

The owl curved off. I stood, too stunned to move
Indoors, or to continue clipping nails.
A bowl of soup boiled over on my stove,
Adding to my more nugatory travails.

Song: "Coast Starlight"

Some days I am so lonely, so content.
The dust lifts up. The trees are weatherbent.
The cypresses lean down against the sea.
The Californian poppies close early.

The poppies close at five. The Coast Starlight
Will get me to the City by tonight,
Will get me to the City and my friend,
Will get me to my month-long journey's end.

The cattle rest among the mustard flowers.
The Starlight circles past the prison towers.
The golfers pull their carts along the green.
The blackbird flies across the deep ravine.

Some days I feel a sadness not of grief.
The shadows lengthen on the earth's relief.
Salinas flows by like a silver shawl.
A girl waves from the ruined mission wall.

Now darkness falls — the moon gives little light.
O Starlight, ride into the gentle night.
O travellers, may starlight see you home.
O travellers, may you not sleep alone.

From California

Sunday night in the house.
The blinds drawn, the phone dead.
The sound of the kettle, the rain.
Supper: cheese, celery, bread.

For company, old letters
In the same disjointed script.
Old love wells up again,
All that I thought had slipped

Through the sieve of long absence
Is here with me again:
The long stone walls, the green
Hillsides renewed with rain.

The way you would lick your finger
And touch your forehead, the way
You hummed a phrase from the flute
Sonatas, or turned to say,

"Larches — the only conifers
That blend honestly with Wales."
I walk with you again
Along those settled trails.

It seems I started this poem
So many years ago
I cannot follow its ending
And must begin anew.

Blame, some bitterness,
I recall there were these.
Yet what survives is Bach
And a few blackberries.

Something of the "falling sunlight",
In the phrase of Wang Wei,
Falls on my shadowed self.
I thank you that today

His words are open to me.
How much you have inspired
You cannot know. The end
Left much to be desired.

"There is a comfort in
The strength of love." I quote
Another favourite
You vouchsafed me. Please note

The lack of hope or faith:
Neither is justified.
I have closed out the night.
The random rain outside

Rejuvenates the parched
Foothills along the Bay.
Anaesthetised by years
I think of you today

Not with impassionedness
So much as half a smile
To see the weathered past
Still worth my present while.

Song: "Waiting"

As I stood on Dolores Street
With thoughts of sadness and defeat
A cat came from across the way
And sat beneath a Chevrolet.

The sun was hot. His grey-green eyes
Surveyed the scene with small surprise.
I plied my pencil furtively.
The cat took no account of me.

I drew the cat with stubby strokes.
I gave the cat appealing looks.
I walked to him. Without demur
He let me stroke his friendly fur.

My friend had gone to run a race.
My heart beat at an urgent pace.
In my mind's eye I saw him breast
The tape, then fall to earth and rest.

I wished that I could touch his hair
And be to him some comfort there,
But here I was, and here the cat,
And there he was, and that was that.

Since when my friend said we would meet
An hour has passed along the street.
The cat purrs in the noonday sun.
O cat, I know my friend has won!

Between Storms

The hills are green again, the lake
Murky. Continual storms
Over California have washed away
Houses, gouged the coastline,
Stranded bewildered seals,
Swept away walkers in aberrant waves
And left a limpness in my brain.
There is no cure —

Except that the light that comes
In the late afternoon after a storm
Enters my room and transfigures
Books, computer print-outs,
The wooden seal the fruitsellers gave me,
And my blue plastic poncho.
Beautiful beautiful light,
Heavy as honey, redolent

Of Cotswold stone
And of lemon groves on drier hills,
Drawing from the heart a music,
Departing suddenly.
Tonight another storm is forecast.
I look out at the two trees,
Uprooted, not yet cleared away,
And hear the squirrels chatter in distress.

And Some Have Madness Thrust Upon Them

Salesmen have come in throughout the day
Bearing photocopying machines into my house.
They have copied graphs onto computer paper,
Bach onto tracing paper,
Academic documents onto sheets of plastic.
Prices have been quoted, reduced.
The more grief-stricken I look, the more they reduce their prices,
And throw in bottles of toner.
I tell them I will think about the matter.

The Toshiba salesman says gently:
"Do yourself a favour — ask the others
If they have selenium drums.
To tell you the truth, those Sharp machines may be cheaper,
But that's because they're cheap. After a thousand copies
They look like dirt." The Gestetner man,
Tight-jawed, grim
— His demonstration machine is being undemonstrative —
Says, "Sure, there's an edge-void, but to be honest,
You'll find that on any machine, and as for the Minolta —
Look — these independent assessments speak for themselves.
I'll leave the machine here for you to . . . no, no, I insist.
You just think about it. It's a steal."

I stare at the Gestetner 2000,
Squat, immovable on my dining table.
I set two places around it
And turn the lights low.
Outside the wind flings itself into the March trees
And I wait for my darling to appear.
I will place the wine on the lid.
It cannot be allowed to come between us.

Spring of Content

Since you have gone, it has grown fresh and still;
The blond hills have turned green, the winter rain
Has pressed the dust back to the earth again.
The ophthalmologist's almond tree is full,
No, swathed with frost-fine blossom, and the scent,
Pressing and light, converts the colourless air;
Grapes of wistaria are everywhere
Usurping walls where climbing roses aren't
Jostling each other in the breeze and sun;
Wild oats and barley intersperse with grass
And boisterous dandelions — and I lie hours
Cat-curled and narcoleptic on the lawn
And think of nothing — not even that you're away
Or that today is — is it? — Saturday.

Moonlight

Some lines from Trakl come to me: moonlight;
His sister plays the sonata once again.
It is as short of hope, as clear with pain.
I listen to the road outside. Despite
Years, despite years, tears blur my steadied sight
Like a bad joke irrelevant words arouse.
Through pylons, as before, the moon tonight
Sears with a fire new time and loves won't douse.

I see some things are much the same. If you
Knocked at my door some year I could not say,
"He lived here once, but now has moved away."
Most things have lost their power to hurt. A few
Exceptions, moonlight, a quintet or two,
May cause these fits to re-occur, but now
I know there is not much that I can do.
I know that they will pass, somehow, somehow.

At any rate I've come to recognize
It's I who built this bleached cairn, stone by stone —
The first time that you spoke to me by phone,
Walks, Wordsworth, woodpeckers, Colombian highs,
The last time that I looked into your eyes:
A derelict memorial on a plain,
Its architect must in time realise
His plan to see beyond his work again.

And as for you, my love of many years,
Who are so fine, quiet and unobsessed,
I wish you what you have already, rest
Of spirit. To you memory appears
Too little worth analysis or tears.
In my heart too I will it not to last,
Nor do I wish that when the moonlight sears
It should inveigle you into the past.

Abalone Soup

Grateful for the resin-scented night
And for the great full moon above the sea
With few remarks we drive to where the light
Brightens the crests of waves tentatively,
Dreaming, while dawn's left hand is in the sky
Of seabed shelves where abalone lie.

Smell of a skunk, coyote on the road,
The redwoods of the coast, a seagull's mew,
Twist to the cove where we now halt to unload
Weights, ab-knives made from leaf-springs, one or two
Yellow string bags to trail the catch to land.
I touch the water and pull back my hand.

They tug their wetsuits on. Jim strips a plant:
"It smells like liquorice." The oval moon,
Squeezed by a fog-bank, loses shape. I can't
— No wetsuit — go with them. "We'll be back soon."
Custodian of their spectacles and keys,
I sit upon the least moist rock and freeze,

Watching them bob and strain to the far rock,
Four buoyant blots against a lightening blue.
Eight thirty. Where are they? At nine o'clock
I'll call up next of kin. "How do you do —
Mrs Gebhart? Your son was lost at sea,
A martyr to cuisine." Ah, abalone,

The gourmet's edelweiss, of the four A's
Of California — asparagus,
Ab, avocado, artichoke — you raise
Our palates to the most vertiginous
Conception of sublimity. . . . But here
Four heads, four snorkels, once again appear.

Beyond the narrow rocks, a stronger swell
Delays the last foray towards the shore,
And now, each twisting in its open shell
Lie sixteen abalone; no, one more.
He is replaced — four abs each is the quota —
Upon a nearby reef below the water.

We climb the hillside on a path between
Wild sweetpea and convolvulus to the car.
One man with cramp (tight beavertail) is keen
On breakfast and on bed. Domestic war
Sputters around a mask and an ab-knife
Lost to the surge. Ah, well, no loss of life —

Or, rather, only sixteen. Beer and Brie
Resuscitate us as we view the catch,
Anticipating oral ecstasy.
Facing the slow Pacific swell we watch
Seven pelicans flap laxly across the sky,
Unperturbed by the traffic blustering by.

Having three times had abalone steak,
Each time with (and by courtesy of) Jim,
Back at his house my pampered tastebuds ache
With lust for ab and gratitude to him.
Once having tasted abalone soup
Little is left to do in life but hope

That Mrs Chen — Jim's Chinese neighbour who,
Though reticent, one evening chanced to see
Him pounding abs in the yard and as he threw
The scraps away, exclaimed, "Give those to me!",
One night appearing with two tureens at the door —
May grant her avid addicts an encore.

Love and Work

The fact is, this work is as dreary as shit.
I do not like it a bit.
While at it I wander off into a dream.
When I return, I scream.

If I had a lover
I'd bear it all, because when day is over
I could go home and find peace in bed.
Instead

The boredom pulps my brain
And there is nothing at day's end to help assuage the pain.
I am alone, as I have usually been.
The lawn is green.

The robin hops into the sprinkler's spray.
Day after day
I fill the feeder with bird-seed,
My one good deed.

Night after night
I turn off the porch light, the kitchen light.
The weight lodged in my spirit will not go
For years, I know.

There is so much to do
There isn't any time for feeling blue.
There isn't any point in feeling sad.
Things could be worse. Right now they're only bad.

Ceasing Upon the Midnight

He stacks the dishes on the table.
He wants to die, but is unable
   To decide when and how.
   Why not, he wonders, now?

A piece of gristle catches his eye.
The phone rings; he turns to reply.
   A smell of burning comes
   From somewhere. Something hums.

The fridge. He looks at it. This room
Would make an unpacific tomb.
   He walks outside. The breeze
   Blows warmly, and he sees

A sky brushed clean of dust and haze.
He wanders in a lucid daze
   Beneath the live-oak tree
   Whose creaks accompany

The drifting hub of yellow light
Low on the hillcrest. Ah, tonight,
   How rich it seems to be
   Alive unhappily.

"O sähst du, voller Mondenschein,
Zum letztenmal auf meine Pein",
   He murmurs to convince
   Himself its force will rinse

The pus of memory from his mind,
Dispel the dust he's swept behind
   The furniture of days,
   And with beneficent rays

59

Kindle the taut and tearless eyes
With the quick current of surprise,
    Joy, frenzy, anything
    But this meandering

Down a dead river on a plain,
Null, unhorizoned, whose terrain,
    Devoid of entity,
    Leads to no open sea.

The moon, himself, his shadow, wine
And Li Bai's poem may define
    A breath, an appetite,
    His link to earth tonight.

He gets a bottle, pours a glass,
A few red droplets on the grass,
    Libation to the god
    Of oak-trees and of mud,

Holds up its colour to the moon,
Drinks slowly, listens to the tune
    The branches improvise,
    Drinks, pours, drinks, pours, and lies

Face down on the moist grass and drinks
The dewdrops off its leaves. He thinks
    Of other moons he's seen
    And creatures he has been.

The breeze comforts him where he sprawls.
Raccoons' eyes shine. A grey owl calls.
    He imitates its cries,
    Chants shreds, invents replies.

The alcohol, his molecules,
The clear and intimate air, the rules
  Of metre, shield him from
  Himself. To cease upon

The midnight under the live-oak
Seems too derisory a joke.
  The bottle lies on the ground.
  He sleeps. His sleep is sound.

Unclaimed

To make love with a stranger is the best.
There is no riddle and there is no test. —

To lie and love, not aching to make sense
Of this night in the mesh of reference.

To touch, unclaimed by fear of imminent day,
And understand, as only strangers may.

To feel the beat of foreign heart to heart
Preferring neither to prolong nor part.

To rest within the unknown arms and know
That this is all there is; that this is so.